Lost Within

BE INSPIRED BY THE IMPORTANCE OF
DEVELOPING A RELATIONSHIP WITH THE LORD

Sylvia Garza

WestBow
PRESS
A DIVISION OF THOMAS NELSON

WestBow Press books may be ordered through booksellers or by contacting:

WestBow Press
A Division of Thomas Nelson
1663 Liberty Drive
Bloomington, IN 47403
www.westbowpress.com
1-(866) 928-1240

Because of the dynamic nature of the Internet, any web addresses or links contained in this book may have changed since publication and may no longer be valid. The views expressed in this work are solely those of the author and do not necessarily reflect the views of the publisher, and the publisher hereby disclaims any responsibility for them.

Book cover designed by Christopher Vela

ISBN: 978-1-4497-8608-3 (sc)
ISBN: 978-1-4497-8609-0 (e)

Library of Congress Control Number: 2013903253

Printed in the United States of America

WestBow Press rev. date: 3/4/2013

THIS BOOK IS DEDICATED FIRST OF all to my Lord, Jesus who inspired, anointed, and imparted in me the gift to write this book.

Also in dedication to my Mother, my mentors Aunts Ermelinda and Sarah

In memory of my Brother Alejandro, my father, my mentors Grandmother Antonia, Aunt Lydia, and Uncle Roberto

Table of Contents

Preface

As I received a call from my sister informing me that our mother was ill, I knew that caring for her would be a journey that I would soon embark upon. Before taking care of her, I knew that I needed to learn about the disease that affected her. Through that journey I knew that it was essential to believe and trust in the Lord. During this journey, my mother faced many challenges because of the Alzheimer's disease. One of the challenges was that she was forgetting her present home and searching for a childhood home. Several times a day she would say she was going home. Then one day I responded, "Mom you are home! This is your house!" She sat on her sofa for a few seconds and began to cry saying, "I feel so lost!" This is a comment that brought tears to my eyes and touched my heart. Her comment will forever stay in my mind and heart.

One day while caring for my mother in Texas my husband called from Michigan to share with me the results of his doctor appointment. My husband was told that he would need open heart surgery in the future. Shortly after, I made a difficult decision to stop caring for my mother. After this we moved to Wyoming. Then a couple of years later while sitting in my living room the Lord said, *"Lost Within."* He said that it was the title of my book. The Lord reminded me of my mother's comment, "I feel so lost!" Because of the journey with my mother this is how *"Lost Within"* was inspired and birthed in me by the Lord. I believe that the Lord asked me to write this book with the purpose of touching the heart of His children. It is my hope and prayer that you would be transformed, encouraged, and inspired because of *"Lost Within."*

Acknowledgement

I WOULD LIKE TO ACKNOWLEDGE AND thank my husband for his patience as I took many hours studying and writing. As a proud mother, my heartfelt thanks to my sons: Noe for his guidance in my story structure, Roberto for his knowledge and advice regarding my preparation before I took this journey, and for Daniel as my personal editor. My deepest thanks to my nephew Christopher as the designer for the book cover. Thanks to my wonderful team for all your support, time, and hard work.

Introduction

LOST WITHIN IS AN INSPIRATIONAL BOOK about getting the Word of God in our hearts. Once it is in your heart you should treasure it and prevent it from becoming suppressed or dormant. It is about the importance of developing a relationship with the Lord and listening to His voice. A relationship that is essential in your walk with God.

The Holy Spirit is a friend that will teach and guide you. One of the many things that He will teach you is about your authority. Praying in that authority can move mountains which can give you an answer to your circumstances. Your prayer is also essential for His people who are recently awakening in exile. You will also encounter the power of weeping.

Lost Within is about relationships, prayer, trust, friendships, love, discipline, healing, encouragement, and as you read you will find much more. It is my hope that it will inspire you to spend time with Him. I pray that you will laugh, cry, learn, and be encouraged upon reading *Lost Within*.

Chapter 1
Lost Within

ONE DAY I RECEIVED A PHONE call from my sister informing me that our mother was ill. I remember thinking that I knew very little about this disease and wondered what was going to happen to her. What is she going to go through? I knew that I needed to educate myself as much as I could about the disease that my mother was stricken with so I could properly care for her. I knew it would help me prepare myself for a season in the future filled with uncertainty and challenges. We do not know what the future holds for us but we can try to prepare as best as possible. With the support of my husband, the time came when I decided to quit my job because she was at a point with her Alzheimer's that necessitated my constant care.

One of the symptoms of this disease is being a wanderer, looking for a childhood place, therefore, always wanting to leave. For this reason, we installed key dead bolt locks. As a wanderer, my mother left the house several times a day saying she was going home. She would go a few doors down to my sister's house and visit for a while. Then she would say to my sister, "I am going home," and would return to her house. Once again she said to me that she was going home but this time I replied, "Mom, you are home. This is your house."

Her response overwhelmed and touched my heart. It brought tears to my eyes and is a comment that I will never forgot. She sat down on her sofa for a few seconds and began to cry then said, "I feel so lost." I assured her that I was here to take care of, love and protect her. You see, my mother was not lost. She just felt lost within herself, at her home, and her surroundings, because of the disease. My mother was unable to recognize her home in her mind but in essence she was not lost.

As time went on I noticed one remarkable thing. As she began to forget names, people, how to cook, and other simple things, I was amazed at the fact that she didn't forget how to pray and lift up her hands to praise her Lord and Savior, Jesus; Yeshua his Hebrew name. This reminds me of the scripture in John 14:26, "But the Helper, the Holy Spirit, whom the Father will send in My name, He will teach you all things, and bring to your remembrance all things that I said to you." I believe the Holy Spirit was helping my mother to remember because in 1987 she confessed Jesus as her Lord according to Romans 10:9 and was water baptized. Being a child of God gave her rights to what the Bible entitled.

Also in Joshua 1:5 it says, "…as I was with Moses, so I will be with you. I will not leave you nor forsake you." I believe that Joshua grabbed hold of this word in his heart because he knew that he was going into battle to possess the land given and promised by covenant to the Israelites by almighty God. For us to remember and grab hold of His Word it would have to be in our hearts which comes by reading the Bible in its entirety. Throughout this time as I cared for my mom we grabbed hold of His Word and knew that He would never leave nor forsake us. He takes care of His children and I could see how He was with us.

One day we decided to clean her closet and as she tried on all her clothes there were skirts that just fell off her. Other clothes were too small and she could not zip or button up. I remember we both began to laugh and laugh. We rolled on the bed laughing and I laughed so hard that my stomach ached. After we stopped laughing I thanked God because in the midst of this disease we were able to find joy. That moment of joy came from the Lord and this is why I know that He watched over us. This is a memory that will stay with me forever.

Knowing that one day she would no longer recognized me as her daughter and not knowing from day to day how she would react when she saw me was why I needed to remember to grab hold of His Word. The time did come when she did not recognize me but praise the Lord that she never seemed afraid around me. She, having forgotten that I was her daughter, made me wonder if she saw me as someone who loved her or someone who could threaten her. I called her mom as often as I could in hopes that it would bring comfort to her. It was an emotional time for me to see my mom forgetting things and I always wondered what she felt when she looked at me.

Well one day she called me the lady of the medicine because she could not remember the word nurse. Remember that at this time in her mind I am a stranger to her. Did she feel scared, confused, alone, hopeless, abandoned, and unsure? I can't begin to fathom what an awful sense it'd be to feel lost within yourself or your home. She was always searching for something or someone, not knowing or realizing that it was all at her fingertips. If she could only remember that I'm her daughter, the one who was there to love and protect her then maybe she could feel comfortable in her surroundings and know that she was in her home. I wonder if at times we feel alone and for a moment we are searching for something or someone. Only to realize that His Word is at our fingertips and all we have to do is call out to the Lord for help. He loves us and is there to protect His children. At this time she was forgetting more words or their meanings so she was not able to grab hold of His Word. Challenging as that may have been, it was up to me to somehow make her feel safe and I truly had to be guided by the Holy Spirit.

Part of the time when I cared for my mom I moved into her home in Texas, again, with my husband's support. During the time that I took care of her I wrote about my mother's actions. I wrote about some of her word pronunciation and phrases. Upon mentioning this to one of my cousins her response was, "you should write a book." One day my husband called from Michigan and said that he was diagnosed with a heart murmur. He was told that in the future open heart surgery would be necessary. I made the decision to move back to Michigan and brought my mother with me. Shortly after this I had to make a very difficult decision to stop caring for my mother because I believed it would have been too challenging to care for both. Soon after, I released her to the care of my sister.

Later in March of 2005 my husband and I moved to Wyoming. Then in the year 2007 while sitting in my living room the Lord spoke to me and said, "Lost Within." He said it was the title of my book. He took me back to the time when my mother said, "I feel so lost." My first thought was, "I am not a writer," and then asked the Lord how and why. I remembered my cousin saying

4

to me that I should write a book. So I began to write a book on Alzheimer's disease but really struggled and could not finish no matter how hard I tried. So at that time I set it aside and forgot about writing.

Between 2005 and 2012 several things had happened in my life. Things that I will talk about later in the book but it was a time for me to trust, learn, and grow in the Lord. I had taught at several churches but at the time I did not know that these teachings were to be part of my book. Then in the summer of 2012 the Lord said, "Lost Within, write the book!" When He said write the book I knew that it had to be written quickly. This time with the guidance of the Holy Spirit I began to write a book not on Alzheimer's but on the Word of God in us. "Lost within" is a book about getting the Word of God in our hearts and not letting it become suppressed or dormant within. It is about the importance of having a relationship with the Lord. This is how "Lost Within" was birthed in my spirit.

I believe that writing this book, with His help, is one way that the Lord wants to touch the lives of many people. Will we continue to grow or will we allow the Word of God to become dormant? One of the Lord's desires is for us to continually have a relationship with Him. How do we build up our spiritual lives? We build our spiritual lives by developing a relationship with Him and some ways to do that is by taking the time to study, read, pray, and fast. When you do not spend time with Him you may feel alone or some other emotions during life's journey. This could happen because of the lack of discipline.

Just as my mother felt lost within herself and in her home, there are people that feel lost when they are walking through their trials. My mother was unable to recognize her surroundings because of the disease so why do we feel lost or unfamiliar in ours? Could it be that the lack of developing a relationship with the Lord or spending time in His Word could cause one to feel lost and not recognize ones surroundings? If only one knew that the answer is just at our fingertips. Yes, it is that simple. Just get on your knees, worship, pray, open the Bible, read, then sit still and listen.

There are still times when I open my Bible to read and do not understand but this does not discourage me from reading. This could be one reason when you are reading the Bible you are, so to speak, in the word but feel lost within it. At times you might not understand a scripture or story in the Bible but the Holy Spirit will bring revelation whether at that moment or in the future through a teaching or person. If I became discouraged because I did not understand something I wondered how I could have had the ability to care for my mother. With daily challenges, not knowing what to expect from her and little sleep some nights, I needed to walk by faith and continually have a relationship with the Lord. I encourage you to press on, keep the faith, and keep reading. It is a daily growth for all of us.

Not all of my prayers have been answered, yet, but this does not discourage me from continuing to pray and believe. Even if we do not understand His answers or timing we still have to trust Him. He is the one that we must run to whether we are in the valley or the mountain top. The more you study His Word the more you get familiar with it and are able to navigate through your trial. When one spends time in His Word it helps you to be familiar with your surroundings and then you are able to grab hold of His Word, just as Joshua did. Be confident that it will carry and sustain you during the times of trouble no matter what it may be. Again, I believe this is important enough to repeat that not taking the time to study and meditate on His

Word along with spending time with Him causes you to become unfamiliar with your surroundings, and that will make you feel lost within.

Preparing before I began to care for my mother was very helpful in understanding what she did and why she said the things she said. I did not go into this situation with my eyes closed or unprepared. How did I prepare? I did two things. One, I spent much time in prayer, fasted, read the Bible and asked the Lord for guidance. Second, I read as much as I could about Alzheimer's disease, spoke with people and organizations. Trials will come because the adversary wants you to fail in life and that is why I believe it is wise to always spend time with the Lord. I wonder how many times we go into life's battles unprepared.

Being unprepared could cause some to feel that they do not know what to do, or out of fear lose sight for a moment during their trial and ask the Lord, "What is happening to me!" or "Why is this happening to me?" Let me share something that happened to me. One day about two months after I confessed Jesus as my Lord the spirit of fear invaded my life and home. Fear will paralyze you as it did me. I remember that I felt someone following me and also felt a breath right behind me. I could not go into any room in my house alone because of fear. I believe that it is during this time when I felt lost within. Why, because I was not familiar with my surroundings, which is His Word, or the ability to navigate His Word.

Fear invaded my life and home for about four months but the way I fought back was in spending time with the Lord and reading His Word. I began by dressing with the armor of God which is His Word. One scripture that I learned is in 1 John 4:4, "You are of God little children, and have overcome them, because

He who is in you is greater than he who is in the world." Then in January of 1988 I received the baptism of the Holy Spirit and with His help I overcame fear and was victorious. Now because of this experience with fear I am very sensitive to fear and danger. I feel a stirring in my spirit when fear in any form is near.

Fear made me feel like I did not have the authority or control of my home or life. I believe that human nature wants to be in control of situations in our own lives. We do everything we can on our own because we want to be in control and at times even before we go to Him in prayer and seek His Word for an answer. Some of us, after the shock, begin to pray and run to the Word of God and seek for an answer. There are others who begin to allow emotions get the best of them. They withdraw or begin to call people for prayer even before they themselves get into their own prayer closet. If one would spend time with Him before trouble comes, then one would less likely feel lost because our first instinct is to run to Him. This relationship is built by spending quality time with Him. Ask the Holy Spirit to lead and guide you.

As I write this book it is my desire to express the importance of reading the Bible and how important it is to develop a relationship with the Lord. Why? Because God provides everything we need in His Word. His armor is spoken in Ephesians 6:10-20 but in verse 12 it says, "For we do not wrestle against flesh and blood, but against principalities, against powers, against the rulers of the darkness of this age, against spiritual hosts of wickedness in the heavenly places." There are different ranks in the military and I believe that everyone has a chance to work their way for advancement. When the spirit of fear invaded my life and home I decided to fight back. How? I used the armor of God and learned strategic scriptures to combat fear. The decision is yours, just as it was mine, to prepare as best as you can. We each decide whether we will work hard to get a promotion. Now let me ask you a couple of questions. What rank would you like to be before you go into battle? How hard are you willing to prepare and train? You know that this takes discipline on your part. Please be encouraged to read all the verses because the Lord does provide a way to prepare for battle not only in these verses but throughout His Word.

Preparing with prayer and fasting before I took care of my mother helped me to have peace and as the Alzheimer's disease progressed in her I knew that the Lord would never leave nor forsake us. I know this for two reasons. First, I placed my trust in my Lord. Second, because one night I had a dream and saw an angel standing at my mother's door guarding her. As one goes through a trial, whatever that may be, know that the same Lord that is with my mother is also with you. Even though my mother lost the ability to praise God, He was never lost within her. Praise God that He has sent His angels to protect us. Praise God that He sent the Holy Spirit to help us. Thank God for His covenant and promises. What an awesome God we serve!

As I end this chapter please allow me to summarize again the importance of developing a relationship with the Lord. The Word has to be in us but for that to happen we must read it entirely, Genesis to Revelation. Reading the Bible is only one way to develop a relationship with the Lord. Therefore I believe that every person should read the whole Bible because then it is in you and once it is in us it will not be lost. Remember that the Holy Spirit will bring it to your remembrance. His Word in 2 Timothy 2:15 says, "Be diligent, another translation says "study", to present yourself approved to God..." Why is the Lord, not me, telling us to be diligent and study? Could it be that He wants us to spend time with Him? Could it be because He wants us to be prepared for battle? So, is His Word lost within us? Of course not! Or are we lost within His Word? I believe that not being prepared causes us to look elsewhere first. It is okay to go to intercessors, family, and friends to help you pray in agreement for victory but one should always run to Him first. I truly believe if you go to Him first, instruction will come and He will place someone in your path to help you. And who knows, it could be a person that will soon become a true friend.

Not being able to navigate or seek an answer in His Word affects our spiritual and prayer life. This speaks volumes about how much time we spend with Him and our relationship with Him. This, in turn, affects our thoughts and speech. Please take the time to read and pray and see how the Holy Spirit will guide you. I know that you will begin to know and hear Him. He is the best friend you could ever have. He created us so that we could have a relationship with Him!

His Word is lost within us in the sense that we neglect to run to it first and to spend time with Him. Therefore I believe because of this neglect His Word becomes hidden, suppressed, or dormant within us. Again, I believe that we need and must go to Him first. In Joshua 24:15 the God of Abraham asked Joshua, "…choose for yourselves this day whom you will serve…" and Joshua responded, "But as for me and my house, we will serve the Lord." What a declaration! So what is your response? Will you trust Him? Will you spend time with Him? I cannot imagine my life without Him so I pray that you choose to serve the God of Abraham as I have. I believe that the title of this book is a cry from the Lord for His people to turn to Him and experience the fullness of who He is in us.

Is prayer lost within you or are you lost within His Word? Do you feel lost within His Word? If you feel lost then ask yourself a question, how much time have I spent with the Lord? It is up to each individual to make a decision and determine whether we will feel lost within His Word. Thank the Lord that it is never too late to start. Start today and experience the fullness of God!

Rise up and prepare for battle!

Chapter 2
Voice of Weeping

As a young girl I remember growing up with a loving father that would take us to the river park for a picnic and swimming. Our father would also take us to the drive-in theater and at times out to have a delicious ice cream cone. These to me were some of the highlights in my childhood. Then as a teenager he began to instill in me to become self-sufficient. He taught me to read a map in order to assist him as we traveled and because of this I am not afraid to get into my car and travel. Other things that he taught me were how to change a tire, oil and filter along with checking spark plugs. He taught me so that if one day I am alone and stranded I would know how to do these things. Because of the things that he taught me I developed a strong will and character. My father cared for our safety but he also wanted us to be strong.

When my oldest son was accepted to college he was also accepted to attend a program that required him to be there for two weeks in the summer. We were so proud and made the trip to drop him off. I remember as we said good-bye I felt, as a mother who was leaving her son, emotional and wanted to cry. I held back the tears because I told myself that I needed to be strong for him. With a strong will it was very difficult to weep especially in the presence of strangers or other people. Weeping to me at times showed weakness but little did I know the truth about weeping. My character allowed little room for weeping so as the Lord began to teach me about it I learned that it was okay to weep.

In January 2012, I received a phone call from one of my sisters asking me to pray because the paramedics were trying to revive my youngest brother. Shortly after, I received a second phone call with the news that my healthy youngest brother had passed away. At that moment I thought, what and how could I pray because I was just told that he was no longer with us. In shock all I could do was to weep and weep in the privacy of my bedroom. I did not know how and why this happened to him but the Holy Spirit reminded me that in 1987 he had confessed Jesus as his Lord and had been water baptized by Pastor Antonia, our grandmother. In the midst of my grief I found comfort in knowing that he's now in heaven.

Before I flew to Texas a pastor asked me if I would teach on a Wednesday night service. At that very moment, because of my grief, I felt that there was nothing in me to teach. I remember looking at him with a heart full of sorrow because I had just lost my brother and responded, if the Lord gives me a new message while I am in Texas then I will teach. I then flew to Texas for the memorial service.

While in Texas I visited my mother who at this time was in the advance stage of Alzheimer's disease and was unable to walk or talk. My mother had only been at this new rehab facility for about six months and had a roommate. Her roommate informed us that she sleeps most nights and at times she hears her mumble in the attempt to talk. When my brother passed away my mother's roommate shared with us that that night she was weeping all night. She knew that her youngest son had passed away. I remember feeling grief and sorrow because I thought how could she express, pray, or voice what was in her heart. How could she be comforted? How was she able to communicate with us or God!

Praise the Lord for giving us different ways to communicate with Him. Romans 8: 26-27 says, "Likewise the Spirit also helps in our weaknesses. For we do not know what we should pray for as we ought, but the Spirit Himself makes intercession for us with groanings which cannot be uttered. Now He who searches the hearts knows what the mind of the Spirit is, because He makes intercession for the saints according to the will of God." This tells me that the Lord knew her heart and heard her weeping. What a comfort to know that through weeping she was able to communicate with Him. One of the things that mothers are called to do is pray for their children. So how could my mother pray? In Romans 8: 27 it says that He searches the hearts so even though my mother could not talk she was still able to pray and share her heart with the Lord because her weeping came from her heart. Thank God that the Spirit knows how and what to pray!

Now let me share a few verses about the heart. Proverbs 27:19 says, "As in water face reflects face, so a man's heart reveals the man." John 7:38 says, "He who believes in Me, as the Scripture has said, "out of his heart, another translation says "belly", will flow rivers of living water." Psalms 119:145 says, "I cry out with my whole heart, hear me, O Lord!" According to Strong's concordance (#'s 2588, 03820, and 2836) the heart is the innermost part of a man and the centre and seat of spiritual life. What I want you to see in these verses is that your prayer should come from your innermost part which is your heart. That is what the Lord searches.

Because of my mother's inability to pray or voice her heart with natural words, she was still able to pour out of her heart with weeping which is a form of prayer. The Lord knew and heard her weeping because it came from her innermost part. When you pray are you praying from your spirit and heart or are you praying from your mind, and memorization of scriptures? Are you able to put aside the hurts and pray for someone from your heart? A man's heart reveals what kind of man he is or we can say that it reveals your prayer. If we truly forgive someone then we should be able to pray from the heart and spirit. I believe that in our weeping we will begin to see more answers to our prayers. Remember, the Lord searches and knows your heart.

While in Texas I heard my cousin share her testimony about a time in her life when her husband had left her with their three children. As a working single mom she was making enough to just sustain herself and her children. Then one day her car needed repairs because of an accident. She was told that it would cost around 2,500 dollars. I remember her saying that this was beyond what she could afford and there was no way she could come up with this amount of money. My cousin said that she went before the Lord, got on her knees, and did not say a word. All she could do was to weep and weep. When she got done weeping she got up and went to work.

As soon as she said that all she could do was weep the Lord spoke to me and said, "That is a form of prayer." I immediately replied to Him saying show and teach me where it says that in the Bible. That led me to begin a search and study of the word weep. This is why in the first chapter I stressed the importance of taking the time to study. I began with the concordance. I looked up and read every scripture on weeping, voice, prayer, and heart. In my studies I found Psalms 6: 6-9. It says, "I am weary with my groaning; all night I make my bed swim; I drench my couch with my tears. My eye wastes away because of grief; it grows old because of all my enemies. Depart from me, all you workers of iniquity; for the Lord has heard the voice of my weeping. The Lord has heard my supplication; the Lord will receive my prayer." I believe that the voices of weeping are your unknown words spoken in prayer to God. Weeping comes from your innermost area, your spirit area, from your heart! One can then say, *"The Voice of my Weeping"* or *"The Words of my Weeping!"* When we pray in the spirit, also known as our heavenly language, or with the voice of our weeping they are unknown words to us but not to the Lord.

Please do not get discouraged or become weary because of an unanswered prayer. We know that through persistence and waiting with expectation that God, who is faithful, will answer you. He always makes a way when there seems to be no way. He cares for you and me. Through my studies I found comfort to know that the Lord knew my mother's heart and heard the prayer from her voice of weeping. He also heard the voice of my cousin's weeping because He answered those unknown words of prayer. Victory was hers because the car was repaired and paid for in full. Little did I know that out of this testimony the Lord would give me this "new message" that I was to teach at the pastor's church in Wyoming. Of course, this message would also be part of this book.

In my studies I found that King David wrote in Psalms 6:8, "...For the Lord has heard the voice of my weeping." One definition for voice is "sounds produced by vertebrates by means of lungs, larynx, syrinx; especially: sound so produced by human beings." Another definition is "a sound resembling or suggesting vocal utterance." A synonym is "say." Therefore I believe that my mother and cousin's weeping were a vocal utterance, a "say." Praise God that He hears and understands our voice of weeping!

As I continued to study I found that the definition for weep means "to express deep sorrow for usually by shedding tears." It is my belief that "to express" would then be a form of communication. This would suggest that if the voice of your weeping is an expression that comes from within your heart then it is heard by the Lord. If it is heard by the Lord, then that implies that the voice of your weeping are unknown spoken words and is a form of spoken prayer.

Your weeping can touch the heart of God as King Hezekiah did. Let's take a look at 2 Kings 20: 1-11. King Hezekiah was told to set his house in order because he was going to die. The story says that he turned his face toward the wall, prayed to the Lord and wept bitterly. The Lord instructed the prophet Isaiah to return and tell Hezekiah, I have heard your prayer, I have seen your tears; surely I will heal you. The Lord extended him 15 years. I believe that God's heart was moved by compassion when He saw and heard Hezekiah's tears and weeping! Isn't that what we want to do, touch the heart of God? King David also knew how to weep before the Lord and see God's heart full of compassion! Jesus expressed a great example especially for men when he wept according to John 11:35. Men, what an opportunity to become a great example through your weeping!

Hannah wept and grieved in her heart because she was unable to conceive a child. This is found in 1 Samuel chapter 1. In verse 10 it says, "And she was in bitterness of soul, and prayed to the Lord and wept in anguish." Then in verse 17 the prophet Samuel said, "Go in peace, and the God of Israel grant your petition which you have asked of Him." Don't wait any longer! Are you ready to receive your petition? Go ahead, let the voice of your weeping be heard and receive your petition.

Another example tells us of a woman, a sinner that washes Jesus' feet which is found in Luke 7:36-50. In this story the woman does not say a word. Her actions speak volumes about her contrite heart. In verse 38 it says, "…and stood at His feet behind Him weeping; and she began to wash His feet with her tears, and wiped them with the hair of her head; and she kissed His feet and anointed them with the fragrant oil." In verse 47-48 the Lord said, "Therefore I say to you, her sins, which are many, are forgiven, for she loved much. But to whom little is forgiven, the same loves little. Then He said to her, your sins are forgiven." Finally in verse 50 it says, "Then He said to the woman, your faith has saved you. Go in peace." Hallelujah, salvation and peace came to her that day.

How will you pray or what is the best way to pray for someone or for a situation? I believe that there are times when you do not need to say anything regarding the situation you are going through or for someone's salvation. All you need to do is intercede in prayer with the voice of your weeping. Praying with your heavenly language and with the voice of your weeping is powerful and effective because this is a time when you are in prayer without being in control. You do not know what words are spoken from your heart and spirit but thank the Lord that He hears and understands. If there are times that you get into your prayer closet and you just cannot say anything, be encouraged to know that it is okay to use your voice of weeping. With weeping we have the ability to touch and move the heart of God.

Finally, in Matthew 15:21-28 the story is about a woman

who cried out to the Lord because her child was severely demon-possessed but Jesus did not say a word to her at this time. What would you do if you were ignored? Would you become discouraged and give up or would you walk by faith with persistence? Here it seems that the disciples are annoyed by her and want her sent away. Will you let someone stand in the way of what is needed? In verse 24 it says, "But He answered and said, "I was not sent except to the lost sheep of the house of Israel." I believe that she took it one step further with her persistence. How desperate do you need an answer to your prayer? Will you be persistent?

Then verse 25-27 says, "Then she came and worshipped Him, saying, Lord, help me!" "But He answered and said, "It is not good to take the children's bread and throw it to the little dogs." Again, with persistence she answered, "...Yes, Lord, yet even the little dogs eat the crumbs which fall from their masters' table." He answered her, "...O woman, great is your faith! Let it be to you as you desire. And her daughter was healed from that very hour." Walking by faith means that at times you must be persistent and not give up. I want the Lord to say to me that great is my faith! Let it be to me as I desire, so what about you?

Throughout the Bible we read that Jesus was moved with compassion and healed the sick. In these four stories that I just shared, you see that they all had different prayer requests but had something in common. Not all were Israelites but they all spoke from their heart! I believe that true weeping is an emotion that will move Jesus to have compassion and that compassion will produce an answer for your prayers. Are you ready to weep from your innermost, your heart and spirit? Get ready to have some of those unanswered prayers, answered!

Ask yourself a question. Is the voice of your weeping coming from your heart and will the Lord answer? King David and King

Hezekiah, did they cry? Hannah and the gentile woman who washed Jesus' feet, did they cry? The gentile woman with a demon possessed child, did she cry? What did they all have in common? Through their voice of weeping, they received answers to their prayers. What would you do if the Lord extended your life by 15 years? If you were unable to conceive and the Lord opened your womb to conceive, how would you train up that child given to you by the Lord? What would you say or not say for forgiveness, salvation and peace? Will you be persistent in your prayer and ask the Lord from your heart no matter what is being said about you? Once you receive your answer, will you continue to serve the Lord and seek Him or will you forget and allow the Word of God to become dormant or lost within you? My prayer is for your life to be changed and transformed so that you would continue to live according to His Word.

God will wipe away our tears according to Isaiah 25:8, Revelation 21:4 and Revelation 7:17. If the Lord takes the time to wipe away your tears that must mean that He listens and cares. Psalms 56:8 says, "You number my wanderings; put my tears into Your bottle; are they not in Your Book?" If tears are in a book, then are they not words? Words are written in a book! In Revelation 5:8 it says, "Now when He had taken the scroll, the four living creatures and the twenty-four elders fell down before the Lamb, each having a harp, and golden bowls full of incense, which are the prayers of the saints."

Revelation 8: 3-4 says, "Then another angel, having a golden censer, came and stood at the altar. He was given much incense, that he should offer it with the prayers of all the saints upon the golden altar which was before the throne. And the smoke of the incense, with the prayers of the saints, ascended before God from the angel's hand." Psalms 141:1-2 says, "Lord, I cry out to You;

make haste to me! Give ear to my voice when I cry (*weep*) out to You. Let my prayer be set before You as incense..." Wow, He wipes, bottles, writes them in a book, hears our prayers and places our tears in golden bowls full of incense! He hears and cares! Go ahead and weep, weep, weep!

When you face the giants, the mountains, and Jericho's walls, in your trials, we sometimes allow the Word of God to become suppressed or dormant because we shift our eyes to the circumstances and problems we face. Sometimes we have to face our circumstances with weeping and remember that when you weep, your prayers are heard and written in a book. Do not allow the Word of God to become suppressed, dormant, or lost within you. His Word is what gets us through different circumstances. It gives us strength, peace, healing, direction, and whatever you are in need of and finally it brings victory! I believe that weeping also brings inner healing.

I believe that the voice or words of your weeping is a higher level of intercession than your native language! Do not stop praying in your native language but what I am encouraging you to do is to add weeping to your prayer life. If praying in the spirit and weeping come from the innermost part, I wonder what you're prophesying. Parents, what will you prophecy and accomplish through your voice of weeping over your children and up to the fourth generation? What will praying with your voice of weeping produce? Will it produce leaders, worshippers, pastors, prophets, psalmist, teachers, mighty warriors, and who knows what else? I believe that praying with your heavenly language or with your voice of weeping, both which come from your spirit, is giving the Holy Spirit total control. How much more can we accomplish using these forms of prayers?

Thank the Lord for giving us different ways to pray when we

do not know how we ought to pray. You can pray in your native language, your heavenly language which is in tongues, mentioned in Isaiah 28:11 and Acts 2:2-4, or you can pray with the voice of your weeping, as King David did in Psalms 6:8. The different ways that He has given us to pray shows His love for us. It is my hope that you will be encouraged to weep more and more knowing that He will hear your heart.

Once again I will ask: Is prayer lost within you or are you lost within His Word? Do you lack the words to prayer? Guess what? The Lord has given you yet another way to pray. It is through your voice of weeping!

Weep, and let the Voice of Your Weeping be heard!

Chapter 3
The Heart of a Champion

MY ABUELA (GRANDMOTHER) WAS A PASTOR and all my life I was raised hearing stories from the Bible. She took every opportunity to share with me the miracles that God performed in her life. She said to me that God was not about religion but about relationships. My abuela did not preach religion, only the Word of God. I will always remember one of her favorite scripture which is in Joshua 1:5 that says, "No man shall be able to stand before you all the days of your life; as I was with Moses, so I will be with you. I will not leave you nor forsake you." What I did not realize at that time is that, through her stories, she was imparting in me the Word of God and I was unknowingly developing the heart of a champion.

About three weeks before my thirtieth birthday, in July of 1987, I confessed Jesus as my Lord. The first two months as a Christian I experienced two things: One, I had a miscarriage. Secondly, the spirit of fear invaded my life and home. I remember thinking, "I am a new Christian. Why is this happening to me?" Why didn't I walk away from God? I believe that it's because of what my abuela imparted in me, my entire life.

The adversary must have not known that a mighty warrior of God had been secretly helping me to develop the heart of a champion. Even though I didn't understand why this was happening to me, I was able, as a young Christian, to heal from the miscarriage and rise up to fight the spirit of fear. Today, I understand this and I pray that you take the time to share your stories and secretly impart them into the lives of those around you.

Victory is declaring and trusting Him regardless of the outcome! Victory is allowing the Lord to have His way! Victory is speaking to your circumstances and declaring that you will not lose your hope, peace, joy and trust in the Lord! Second Timothy 4:7-8 says, "I have fought the good fight, I have finished the race, I have kept the faith. Finally, there is laid up for me the crown of righteousness, which the Lord, the righteous Judge, will give to me on the Day, and not to me only but also to all who have loved His appearing." Victory is running your race knowing that you have done your best! That is obtaining the heart of a champion!

The heart of a champion is also built and developed through the trials in your life along with reading the Bible. As fear invaded my life and home I decided to fight back as a warrior. As a result of that trial, I continued to develop and strengthen in me the heart of a champion. By praying, reading, and spending time with the Lord, it helped me to grow spiritually and be victorious. These trials in our lives are what people refer to as walking in the wilderness. I believe that this is a time in our lives when the Lord is helping us to mature and develop character. It is not a time that we always enjoy but I believe that there is a purpose for being in the wilderness. Do you want to develop the heart of a champion? Then take the time to listen to the voice of God and the guidance of the Holy Spirit.

When someone feels like they are in the wilderness of life they must seek God with all their heart. As I picture what a wilderness and desert look like, I see the wilderness as nature full of things to help us survive. There are berries, mushrooms, trees, rivers, streams, fish and many other survival provisions. These provisions are placed there by the Lord. We stand there and contemplate what we need to survive instead of asking the Lord what we should use. I believe that at times we focus on the provisions to help us get through our situation instead of the provider who is God almighty. This leads me to believe that in the wilderness we can still choose to take care of ourselves and control our situation.

My husband enjoys hunting and being outdoors. He is an avid hunter and has been hunting since he was around twenty years of age. One day his friend invited him to go scout an area for elk but before they left they prayed for a safe and productive trip. Upon arriving at the wilderness area he set the way point on his GPS but what he did not realize is that he forgot to push the button a second time to save the way point. They began to hike towards Singer Peak to look for any evidence of elk sign. The hike took them approximately four hours one way.

After lunch they decided that it was time to return to the truck. When my husband looked at his GPS he realized that he had not saved the way point. They knew the general direction so they began to hike back. He knew that the truck was near a road that ran east and west but in actuality it ran northeast. Because they were relying on their own ability they did not know that the path took them past the truck. They did not have any more food supplies then realizing that nightfall was approaching they began to feel nervous. At this time they decided that they needed to stop walking and pray. Now that it was dark my husband thought that they had gone too far so they turned around and headed back again. Earlier in the day they felt that they had control of the situation because they had food supplies, sunshine, GPS and were a little familiar with the surroundings. At this time there was no need to pray. Now without the GPS, food supplies and sunshine they knew that they needed the Lord's help to find the truck. Thank the Lord that they found their way and returned home safely.

As you can see that at the beginning of the hike they were in control of their situation, but by the end of the hike God was. There comes a time in the wilderness when we are backed up against a wall. This is when we run to Him for help and give Him control of our circumstances. I'm not saying that this always happens or that it's what everyone does, but it's something that I've occasionally have done myself. The wilderness has some provision that we can use so I see it as a place where we sing, dance, and praise the Lord. Because you are depending on the provisions in the wilderness, could it be that this is a time in our life when we slack off and not read, pray, or spend time with the Lord on a daily basis? The environment in the desert is totally different therefore we must totally depend on the guidance of the Holy Spirit.

As I picture the desert in my mind I see sand in all directions with the heat of a very hot sun. It is this heat that describes the seriousness of your situation. I see the desert as a place where you have no control and you must walk by faith. Other than the rising and setting of the sun you have no idea or sense of direction. I think that it is like having a blind fold on then asked to walk outside and placing your trust in a person to guide you. Thank the Lord for giving us the Holy Spirit because this is where we must totally depend on His guidance. It is a place where your steps must be ordered by the Lord and you completely trust Him. As He orders your steps I believe that He will direct you to the oasis! In the midst of all that sand and hot sun, yes, God has provided for us a survival place called an "Oasis!" I believe that the desert is a place when all you can do is to bow down, fall on your knees and worship Him. Could it be that this is a time in our lives when we read, pray, fast, and spend time with Him?

When I was a young girl our father took us to Traverse City to work in the fields. One day he told us that we would go to the beach and relax. I remember that our parents told us, for safety reasons, to go ahead as a group because the way there was all sand. They also told us that they would soon follow and join us. Our cousins, my brothers, sisters, and I began to hike towards the beach. Half ways there I decided that I wanted to return to the camp with my parents. Upon returning by myself I could not find the same trail back. I found myself going back to reach the kids then turning back to join my parents. I did this several times that by the time I knew it, I was lost and off the original path. I felt lost within that short area when I kept going back and forth. Then I finally stood still and cried. Then as my parents were on the way to the beach they saw me at a distance and rescued me.

Because there was sand all around me I did not have a sense of direction. As a young girl I did not think to pray. All I did was to stand still and cry but standing still is what saved me. There are times in life when you feel like you are in the desert and the best thing to do is stand still and worship Him. Today I know to stand still, pray, worship and wait on the Lord. How would I know that? I know this because I have taken the time to read and study His Word. I found that Psalm 46:10 says, "Be still, and know that I am God..."

Being in the wilderness or desert can at times feel like you are lost. You feel lost because you do not know which direction to go. Maybe you are not lost but just need direction. The wilderness or desert is a time to stop and listen to God. So maybe it is not a time of feeling lost but a time of being lost in Him. We need to be lost in Him so that we can find ourselves or to receive instruction and direction. It should be a time that you spend in praise and worship. You sing, dance, and praise the Lord in the wilderness but you bow down and worship Him in the desert.

When you do not read, pray, or spend time with Him daily, not only will His Word seem lost within you but you run the risk of famine. The wilderness and desert are a place where this could also happen. Disobedience is also another reason why famine can be evident in your life. One definition for famine is "a drastic shortage" "acute shortage of anything" "severe hunger." A shortage of anything could be a spiritual lack or hunger. How do we reach the state of severe spiritual hunger? How do you become drastically short or severely hungry for His Word? By not disciplining your life according to what the Lord is asking of you. If you read the Bible you will find out what He requires of you. It is a book of teaching, instruction, guidelines, principles, and much more. Please discipline yourself and do not neglect your walk with Him.

We should discipline ourselves and not take it for granted that we will always have the freedom to pick up our Bibles to read. In the Bible, Amos speaks about spiritual famine. It is in chapter 8 verses 11 and 12. It says, "Behold, the days are coming," says the Lord God, that I will send a famine on the land, not a famine of bread, nor a thirst for water, but of hearing the words of the Lord. They shall wander from sea to sea, and from north to east; they shall run to and fro, seeking the word of the Lord, but shall not find it." According to the book of Amos the time will come when we will not hear the words of the Lord. When that time comes then because you took the time to put His Word in your heart no one can take it away. Talk about trusting and hearing the voice of the Holy Spirit to guide you. Are you ready for such a time?

The different definitions for champion are "warrior, fighter" "a militant advocate or defender" "one that does battle for another's rights or honor <God will raise me up a champion — Sir Walter Scott>." "a winner of first prize or first place in competition; also: one who shows marked superiority <a champion at selling>."

A champion is a winner if they are competing, but we as children of God are not competing. We are not competing but we are already winners because when we go home to be with the Lord, we win! The heart of a champion requires really only one thing: To be a warrior or fighter. We are in battle with the adversary therefore we are warriors. So as warriors we must prepare for battle. Suit up and put on your armor provided by the Lord according to His Word in Ephesians chapter 6. For 1 John 4:4 says, "You are of God, little children, and have overcome them, because He who is in you is greater than he who is in the world."

I pray that you would rise up and walk with a heart of a champion. May you hunger and thirst for more of Him. I ask the Lord to feed your hunger and quench your thirst. Psalm 37: 19 says, "They shall not be ashamed in the evil time, and in the days of famine they shall be satisfied." Lord, be their source during any form of famine. I pray oh Lord that You would stir and place a desire in their hearts to seek a deeper walk in Your Word and a desire for a deeper walk in knowing You which will cause them to walk victorious as warriors and not in famine. Amen!

Arise as warriors with the Heart of a Champion and prepare for battle!

Chapter 4

Awakening in Exile

On a sunny spring Michigan afternoon I decided to sit in the family room with a cup of coffee and watch television. As I was surfing the channels I saw a Hispanic man on the Christian channel. He was speaking about his ancestors and heard him use the term Sephardic Anusim. He said Sephardic Anusim included Hispanic Jews. It quickly grabbed my attention so I began to listen carefully. I remember thinking to myself that this could not be possible. At the conclusion of the program he gave a website where we could read on this topic.

After the program was over I read an article then called two of my aunts. My aunt Melin listened and asked me to send her a copy of the article. I re-read the article with skepticism then sent it to her. My aunt Sarah listened and then encouraged me to learn what I could about this topic. At this time I knew that I needed to process this information and go to the Lord in prayer. For now I decided that I would not proceed with any search.

At that time my husband and I lived in Michigan but in 2005 we moved to Wyoming. Then around 2007 I heard that a rabbi from Colorado was going to speak at the local synagogue. I attended the meeting and to my amazement he began to speak about the Hispanic Sephardic Anusim. I remember crying and saying to myself this is the second time I have heard this. Could this be a coincidence and could we be such a hidden people? I asked a Jewish couple sitting next to me if they believed in coincidence and they said no. Then I asked, "Why would God send me to Wyoming if my lineage was from Texas and Mexico?" They both responded in immediate harmony saying, "frontiering." What came across my mind was "frontiering what?"

They encouraged me to speak with the guest rabbi. As I was speaking with him and his wife I remember trying very hard to hold back my tears. He said, me being here was not a coincidence and encouraged me to search my family tree. Leaving the meeting with so many emotions and questions I thought to myself about how difficult it would be to begin a search for my family tree. Then I convinced myself that I did not know where or how to begin my search. Because of my curiosity, I began to read a little here and a little there but without passion in my heart. Again, I decided not to proceed with any real determination for my heritage.

Then one day I heard that one of my cousins was moving to Montana. She was the daughter of my aunt who just listened and did not comment when I shared with her about the program and article. This cousin heard about a conference which was going to be held in Denver. My aunt told her to invite me to go to this conference because she remembered that I was interested about Sephardic Anusim. Her and her family came and spent a couple of nights with us. It was at this time when I learned that they had embraced Judaism and had begun to search their Jewish lineage.

My aunt Sarah, in all her wisdom, did not say anything at first because she wanted me to be led by the spirit of God. She later shared with me that she did this so no one could say that I was just following them in their own search.

The next day we drove to the conference and to my amazement the guest speaker was the same man that I heard speaking on the Christian channel. At the conference I found myself captivated by the amazing stories, history, and facts about Sephardic Anusim. This was the third time that I heard on this topic. Upon returning home after listening to this speaker I found it difficult to sleep. I tossed and turned most of the night because my mind kept wandering. All I could think about was the information I had just heard. He had some very convincing facts and we were awestruck upon listening to him.

I awoke around three in the morning but did not get up for fear of making noise that would awaken my cousin and her family. That morning as my cousin and I were talking she told me that she too had been awake since about three in the morning. As we discussed what we had heard I realized that she was just as captivated by this information. I believe what seemed to be lost within and hidden in our ancestors was being stirred in me by the Lord. That night I began to feel a great tug, pulling and urgency in my heart to search for the truth about our ancestors. Even though my cousin's family had already embraced Judaism and been searching their heritage she also had a great tug and urgency in her heart to continue. This time I made the decision to begin my search both in mine and my husband's family heritage.

As I began to research, I found many similarities. My research included foods, names, customs, traditions, locations, and listening to family stories including the way my grandfather and father butchered an animal. As a young child I used to play dominoes with my grandfather, my mother's dad. During those times he would tell me stories about his family. One story that he shared with me was about how his family came from Spain in a ship. My thought as a young child was that this could not be true. He was born in Mexico therefore all of his family was from Mexico. Please be encouraged to ask your parents and grandparents to share family stories with you. In those fascinating stories you could begin to uncover family history.

At this time it was still hard to believe that there was a possibility that we were from Jewish lineage. During the research my husband and I began to attend classes at the local synagogue. We were amazed at some of the history and stories that the rabbi was teaching because it was similar to how we were raised. One thing that she said was that some Jews cover the mirrors when a loved one passes away. I recall my husband saying, "I saw some family member doing that but I did not know why." After much research we believed and learned that, yes, we were of Jewish lineage. To confirm what we had learned my husband had a DNA test and found that his parents were indeed Jewish. I have also found that my grandfathers were Jewish.

Due to the results of our findings I would like to focus on the Hispanic Sephardic Anusim. These findings sparked an interest to begin reading as much as we could regarding this topic in great depth. According to Wikipedia it says, "Sephardi Jews is a general term referring to the descendants of Spanish and Portuguese Jews who lived or live in the Iberian Peninsula. This term essentially means "Spanish". It comes from Sepharad, a Biblical location. This location is disputed, but "Sepharad" was identified by later Jews as the Iberian Peninsula, and still means "Spain" in modern Hebrew."

According to the Jewish Encyclopedia, "in 1274 Bertrand

de la Roche was appointed inquisitor of Judaizing Christians in Provence, and in 1285 William of Auxerre was nominated inquisitor for heretics and apostatizing Jews. About 1276 several backsliding converts were burned by order of Nicolas III.; thirteen Jews were burned as heretics in 1288 at Troyes; and at the auto da fé held at Paris March 31, 1310, a converted Jew who had returned to Judaism also died at the stake."

It also stated that, "The New or Spanish Inquisition, introduced into the united kingdoms of Castile, Aragon, and Navarre by Ferdinand V. and Isabella the Catholic, was directed chiefly against converted Jews and against Jews and Moors. During the cruel persecutions of 1391 many thousands of Jewish families accepted baptism in order to save their lives. These converts, called "Conversos," "Neo-Christians" ("Christaõs Novos"). or "Maranos," preserved their love for Judaism, and secretly observed the Jewish law and Jewish customs."

"After the discovery of the New World, Spain introduced the Inquisition into her American colonies, and proceeded against the Maranos and Jews who had sought refuge there. One of the first to be condemned by the Inquisition at New Española was Diego Caballero, the son of Neo-Christians from Barrameda. The Inquisition was introduced into Mexico in 1571; and three years later the first auto da fé was held."

As we read as much as possible we found that some of our ancestors came to Mexico by ship from Spain. My grandfather's stories are true! It seems that according to history many Jews in Spain were given an ultimatum from the Inquisition to convert or face persecution, torture and be killed. Because of this ultimatum many were forced into exile to find refuge. Others chose to convert and became Catholics. Although many who chose to convert secretly observed their customs and lied about their conversion in order to survive and avoid death. This decision forced many to teach their children to stay quiet about their heritage and keep their identity as a secret. One story that my aunt Melin told me was that her father, my grandfather, would not open up to discuss his family history. Thank God that shortly before he passed away he did share names of family members with my aunt. I believe because of this the Torah and Jewish customs became hidden in their hearts. Eventually it also became suppressed and dormant within the future generations. Now after many years the Torah seemed lost within their and our hearts.

I believe that this is why today we and many others did not know our true heritage. There are others who yet need to find their lineage. Thank God that He is in control and the covenant still stands. To be suppressed or dormant does not mean that it is lost or forgotten but asleep which in essence is not lost within. I wanted to know what the Lord had to say and how it affected us today. This also led me to read the Bible and related Jewish and Christian information.

Obadiah 1:20 says, "And the captives of this host of the children of Israel shall possess the land of the Canaanites as far as Zarephath. The captives of Jerusalem who are in Sepharad shall possess the cities of the South." Sepharad is Spain according to Wikipedia. I once again recalled my grandfather's story. This story touched my heart to see and read the Bible with different lenses. I felt like I became part and jumped into the pages of the Bible. It became alive and personal for me. Today, the Sephardic Anusims are a people awakening in exile!

It is my understanding that Moses wrote in the Torah what would happen to the Israelites if they would be obedient or disobedient. I believe that exile is the people's choice or decision because of their disobedience in their walk with God. God never breaks His covenant or promises. Throughout Bible history we find that the Israelites go into exile because they walked away from the purpose that they agreed to do on Mount Sinai. We see that they break the promise made on Mount Sinai which causes their enemies to attack and this eventually leads them into exile. Many eventually prospered while in exile that they decided to stay and not return to Israel. I believe that this causes the possibility of the Torah to seem lost within them. The Torah is not lost within them but I believe that it becomes suppressed or dormant.

Because there is so much information about this topic I encourage you to begin your own reading. If you read the Bible you will learn that the Jews were scattered into many different nations. Whatever your background it is my hope that you will begin to search your own family tree history. If I had not researched it I would have never known that our ancestors lived beyond Mexico. Where do your ancestors come from? Also there is so much in the Bible that I again encourage you to read it over and over again because every time you read it you will find something you missed or something new.

That which seemed to be hidden, dormant, suppressed or lost within is being awakened in us today. I believe that it is in God's plan to awaken the Torah within His hidden people. Praise the Lord that the Sephardic Anusim are finding that the Torah which seemed lost within is coming alive in them. Praise the Lord that many are also embracing Judaism and their customs. Many are already finding their heritage and ancestry linked to a people chosen by God known as Hebrews. My husband and I are such hidden people. We are a remnant that is awakening in exile.

Chapter 5
Echo of Voices

THE ECHO OF OUR VOICE WILL be determined by the decisions we make each day. These decisions mold, shape, and build character in us. You know what is good or bad. Your choose life or death, to be obedient or disobedient and make other decisions in life. When you choose to build a relationship with the Lord you begin to recognize His voice. The Holy Spirit is there to teach and guide when you read the Bible. He will always guide you in the right direction. Praying and reading the Bible is a good decision because it is one way to communicate with Him. When you chose to praise and worship Him then you get closer to Him. We might feel lost within because we made a decision to neglect our relationship with Him. Choose you this day whom you will serve! What echo do you want people and your family to hear?

Why read the Bible and study? Why develop a relationship with the Lord? One should read, study, and spend time with the Lord because He has provided all that we need in the scriptures.

He provides finances, healing, restoration, household salvation, or whatever else you require. The heart and character of God is in the Word of God. Here are some of His characteristics that you will see: love, compassion, mercy, faithfulness, peace, strength, and joy. There are many other attributes of God that you will also see as you read the Bible. You will read stories about love, healing, friendship, salvation, joy, war, peace, family, and many different adventures. My prayer is for the Word of God to forever echo in your life and heart.

Men, Proverbs 21:1 says, "The king's heart is in the hand of the Lord, like the rivers of water; He turns it wherever He wishes." Please ask the Lord to direct your path. It also says in Proverbs 25:2, "It is the glory of God to conceal a matter, but the glory of kings is to search out a matter." Be encouraged that every time you study and search the Word of God know that He will reveal it to you. Proverbs 27:19 says, "As in water face reflects face, so a man's heart reveals the man." Let your light within you shine everywhere you go. Also in Proverbs 18: 22 it says, "He who finds a wife finds a good thing, and obtains favor from the Lord." And finally in Proverbs 31:23 it says, "Her husband is known in the gates, when he sits among the elders of the land." I believe that one way men are known is because of their involvement and by helping in the church or synagogue they attend.

As men are the leaders and kings of their homes, my prayer for you is that you would arise and be led of the Lord. May you seek and search the Lord with all your heart and let people see the light of Jesus in you. As you serve the God of Abraham, Isaac, and Jacob one way to show the love of God in you is to treat your wife as a queen and in doing so you will obtain favor from the Lord. Teach and pray for your children. Mighty warriors of the Lord may you run your race and may your voice echo forever!

Women, Proverbs 12: 4 says, "An excellent wife is the crown

of her husband." I encourage all women to also read Proverbs 31: 10-31 because it speaks about a virtuous wife. Women rise up, pray and worship the God of Abraham, Isaac, and Jacob. Support your husband and be the glue that keeps everything together. The women are the ones who create the atmosphere in the home. What kind of atmosphere have you created in your home? Teach, train up, and pray for your children. Let all those you come in contact with see that you do walk as a virtuous woman. May your strength be seen as you walk in humbleness and meekness! Virtuous women of the Lord, run you race and may your voice echo forever!

Isaiah 40:8 says, "The grass withers, the flower fades, but the word of God stands forever." My final thought to you is for you to know that the Word of God does not fade, change, nor is done away with but stands forever. For He is the same yesterday, today, and forever according to Hebrew 13:8. I encourage you to read the entire Bible and let it get rooted deep inside you so that it will never become suppressed, dormant, or lost within you. Please know that He is awesome and we serve a great and mighty, loving God! Let His Word echo in you!

Today, as some of my mentors walk the streets of gold according to Revelation 21:21c, I will forever remember and hear their voices echo in my life. As the voices of my mentors echo, I recall the last words that my Uncle Roberto, pastor, said to me, *"What the Lord has given and revealed to you, grab hold of it, run with it, and don't let anyone take it away!"* He loved to sing about the faithfulness of God. The "Faithfulness of God" was his favorite message to teach. The first lesson that my Abuela (grandmother) taught me was, *"One thing that you always must do is to be obedient to the Lord!"* The voices of my mentors will continue to echo in my life as I remember their favorite scriptures. My Abuela - Joshua 1:5, Joshua 1:9, and Jeremiah 33:3; my Uncle Roberto – Isaiah 55:6 and my Aunt Lydia – Philippians 4: 13 and as a worshipper her family sing some of her favorite songs. They are (Spanish version) "Todo lo bueno que tengo lo he recibido de Dios. Me ha dado todo en su gracia, me ha dado todo en su amor." (All of the good that I have I have received from the Lord. He has given me all in His grace; He has given me all in His love.); Un rio me mostro; Tierra Bendita (Blessed Land). This song is a song about blessing Israel. They will forever be remembered!

Today I continue to receive from my mentors and these are their favorite scriptures: my Aunt Melin – Proverbs 3:6, Psalm 27:4, and Psalm 20:1-9; my Uncle Ramiro - Joshua 1:5 and Joshua 1:9; my Aunt Sarah – Psalm 103:1-2 and Isaiah 33: 17.

Prayer of Salvation: I invite anyone who has not yet confessed Jesus, Yeshua His Hebrew name, as their Lord to do so now according to Romans 10:9. Pray: Jesus, I am a sinner and I need a Savior. I ask you to come into my heart and be my Lord and Savior. Amen! Welcome to the family of God!

These are some scriptures that I pray in my prayer closet. It is a starting point for anyone who is just beginning to read the Bible. My hope is that the word of God continues to echo in your life as you read and memorize these and other Bible scriptures.

Jeremiah 1:5

> Before I formed you in the womb I knew you;…

Romans 10: 9

> That if you confess with your mouth the Lord
> Jesus and believe in your heart that God has raised
> Him from the dead, you will be saved.

Acts 16:31

> So they said, "Believe on the Lord Jesus Christ and you will be saved, you and your household."

Psalm 68: 5

> A father of the fatherless, a defender of widows, is God in His holy habitation.

Joshua 1:5

> No man shall be able to stand before you all the days of your life; as I was with Moses, so I will be with you. I will not leave you nor forsake you.

Joshua 24: 15

> ...choose for yourselves this day whom you will serve,...
> ...But as for me and my house, we will serve the Lord.

2 Chronicles 7: 14

> If My people who are call by My Name will humble themselves, and pray and seek My face, and turn from their wicked ways, then I will hear from heaven, and will forgive their sin and heal their land.

Psalm 34:15

> The eyes of the Lord are on the righteous, and His ears are open to their cry.

Psalm 34:17

> The righteous cry out, and the Lord hears, and delivers them out of all their troubles.

Psalm 46: 7 & 11

> The Lord of hosts is with us; the God of Jacob is
> our refuge.

Psalm 55: 22

> Cast your burden on the Lord, and He shall
> sustain you; He shall never permit the righteous
> to be moved.

Psalm 91:11

> For He shall give His angels charge over you, to
> keep you in all your ways.

Proverbs 3: 5 & 6

> Trust in the Lord with all your heart, and lean
> not on your own understanding; in all your ways
> acknowledge Him, and He shall direct your
> paths.

Proverbs 4: 23

> Keep your heart with all diligence, for out of it
> spring the issues of life.

Proverbs 22: 6

> Train up a child in the way he should go, and
> when he is old he will not depart from it.

Isaiah 53 (is speaking of Jesus (Yeshua) the Messiah of Israel)

> Vs-5 says that He was wounded for our
> transgressions, He was bruised for our iniquities;
> the chastisement for our peace was upon Him,
> and by His stripes we are healed.

Isaiah 55:11

> So shall My word be that goes forth from My mouth; it shall not return to Me void, but it shall accomplish what I please, and it shall prosper in the things for which I sent it.

Matthew 8: 16 & 17

> When evening had come, they brought to Him many who were demon-possessed. And He cast out the spirits with a word, and healed all who were sick, that it might be fulfilled which was spoken by the Isaiah the prophet, saying: "He Himself took our infirmities and bore our sicknesses."

1 John 5: 4

> For whatever is born of God overcomes the world. And this is the victory that has overcome the world – our faith.

Walk by faith and let your voice echo!

Bibliography

Chapter 1 – Lost Within
NKJV Study Bible, Second Edition; New King James Version, Copyright 1982 by Thomas Nelson,Inc., Print, pages: 1689, 1783, 328, 2011, 1868-1869, 1927, and 364
http://www.biblegateway.com/passage/?search=2%20Timothy+2:15&version=KJV

Chapter 2 – Voice of Weeping
NKJV Study Bible, Second Edition; New King James Version, Copyright 1982 by Thomas Nelson,Inc., Print, pages: 1779, 1002, 1673, 941, 824, 602, 1682, 419, 1608-1609, 1514-1515, 1076, 2060, 2040, 873, 2037, 2040, 955, 1080, and 1709
http://www.biblestudytools.com/lexicons/greek/kjv/kardia.html
http://www.biblegateway.com/passage/?search=John+7:38&version=KJV
http://www.biblestudytools.com/lexicons/hebrew/kjv/leb.html
http://www.biblestudytools.com/lexicons/greek/kjv/koilia.html

http://www.merriam-webster.com/dictionary/voice
http://www.merriam-webster.com/dictionary/weep

Chapter 3 – The Heart of a Champion
NKJV Study Bible, Second Edition; New King James Version, Copyright 1982 by Thomas Nelson,Inc., Print, pages: 328, 1930, 864, 1402, 1868-1869, 2011, and 855
http://www.merriam-webster.com/dictionary/champion

Chapter 4 – Awakening in Exile
http://en.wikipedia.org/wiki/Sephardi_Jews
http://www.jewishencyclopedia.com/articles/8122-inquisition
NKJV Study Bible, Second Edition; New King James Version, Copyright 1982 by Thomas Nelson,Inc., Print, page: 1408

Chapter 5 – Echo of Voices
NKJV Study Bible, Second Edition; New King James Version, Copyright 1982 by Thomas Nelson,Inc., Print, pages: 993, 999, 1002, 990, 1008, 979, 1008, 1097-1098, and 1966

About the Author

Sylvia Garza wrote and taught a curriculum to the second graders at the church her and her family attended in Michigan. Sylvia and her husband also ministered as head greeters. They moved to Wyoming and at that time she began to teach at different churches. They have three wonderful children and live in Cheyenne, Wyoming.

Printed in the United States
By Bookmasters